13 Years of Thoughts: A Book of Poetry©

by Galilea Valverde
Illustrated by: Resha Hanson

Coffee Seed Books' Publishing
Arlington, WA
coffeeseedbooks.com

Published by Coffee Seed Books' LLC, USA, Arlington, WA 98223
www.coffeeseedbooks.com

Written by: Galilea Valverde
Illustrated by: Resha Hanson. Designed by: Cristina Masterjohn. Edited by: Malva Izquierdo

Library of Congress Control Number: 2023921097
Thirteen Years of Thoughts: A Book of Poetry/ Valverde, Galilea.
Coffee Seed Books' Publishing 12/31/2023
Created in the United State of America.
ISBN:978-1-943718-89-4 (SC). 978-1-943718-90-0 (eBook).

Thank you to everyone involved in creating this book!

Please share your opinion about this book on your preferred
social media platform or book retailer website. Thank you!

To my father, mother, and sisters, Camila and Natalia,
who have helped my spark of creativity become a flame. -GV

POEMS

To My Father

The wise words you give me, like a river flow.

Your kindness is like the soft breeze that blows.

Like a tree, your years grow and grow.

And closer comes the day that I will have to go,

But I will be confident, because you have given me everything I know.

ANIMAL POEMS

Armadillo

With armor made of dust and stone,
You scurry through the desert sands,
Finding a place to rest your head.
You are a warrior without a home.

7

Bear

With mouth wide open and eyes shining bright,
It prowls endlessly throughout the night,
Eating food from berry to man, enjoying every bite.

Beetle

Black to gold, green to pink,
All the rainbow on one bug.
It's so silly to think.

11

Chameleon

From brightest yellow to deepest blue,
You hide in plain sight, sticking your tongue out too.
So fast, no wonder that bug never again flew.

Bunnies

Hop, hop, sniff, sniff, twitch, twitch.
When I pet you please don't flinch.
Coat of sugar white and muddy brown,
Fluffy and furry, you don't make a sound.
Little and small,
Not big or tall.
Lick my hand or my cheek
And I will give you a sweet treat.
My furry pet, my tiny friend,
I will love you 'til the end.

Crab

Scuttle, *wuddle*, wibbly.
That's the sound you make as you go.
Scuttle, *wuddle*, wibbly.
Angrily sand you throw.
Scuttle, *wuddle*, wibbly.
Ouch! You pinched my toe.

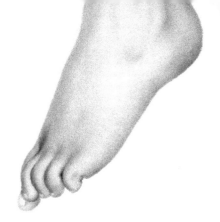

17

Desert Creature

Camel, camel in the sand,
Walking proudly across the land,
Carrying silk and spice for the caravan.

19

Cat and Mouse

Lurking in the shadows the meadow stands still.
The predator moves with so much skill.
Fear is running through my veins,
All the courage from me drains.
The killer's coat is as dark as night,
Its eyes are yellow and very bright.
It has a heart as cold as stone.
It hears my fear rattling through my bones.
It loves fresh meat,
It is ready to eat.
I run and I run, I cannot go far.
For it is quicker than a shooting star.
A killer hidden in the dark, impossible to see,
But I feel its breath over me.
Death is right around the bend,
It's ready to pounce, this is the end.

21

Crocodile

Toughest scales you've ever seen,

Eyes of deepest emerald green.

Powerful tail, strong and true.

Claws of purest sapphire blue.

You won't know she's in the mud,

Until her jaws are stained with your ruby red blood.

Jellyfish

Many spots,
Many stripes.
To some it brings beauty,
To some it brings fright.
Swimming freely
Day and night.

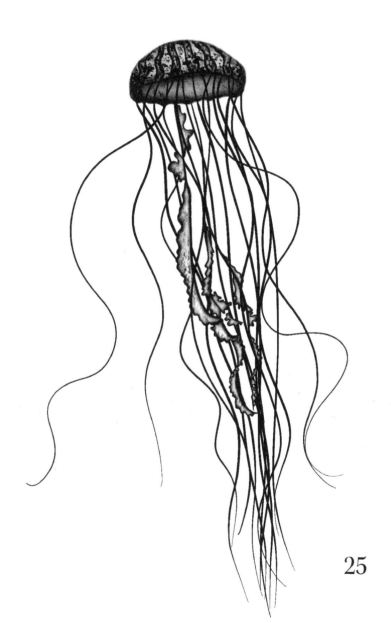

25

Lion

Like a good leader he's gentle and kind,
Something no one pays any mind.
If you make him mad you'll find
He strikes fast and leaves no bones behind.

School of Fish

A strange all-seeing rainbow
Swimming quickly across the sea,
Moving in perfect harmony.

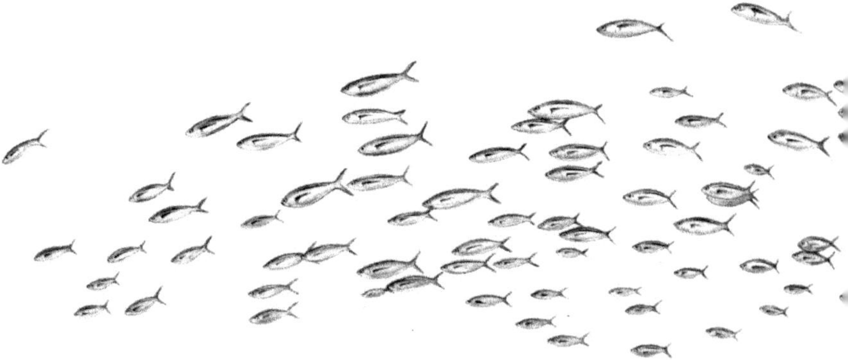

Small Fish

One small fish
Travels the sea.
Its purpose to bring
Color and joy to you and me.

Whale

A tongue, some flippers, and a tail.
All of this makes up a whale.

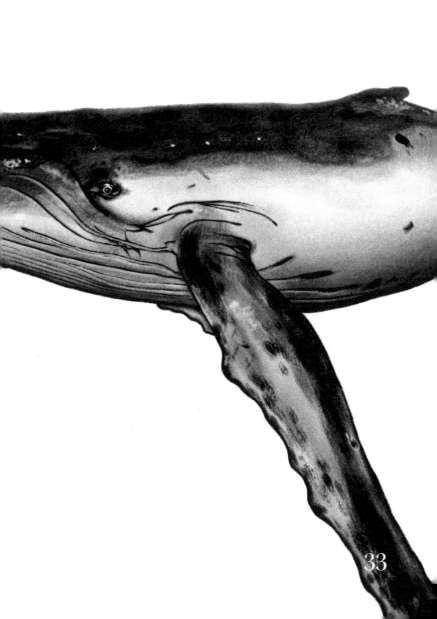

33

HUMAN FEELINGS

What's to Come?

I realized life is simply waiting for what's to come.
One thing is for sure, in the end, not all is said and done.
For some, life is short, for others it is long.
But they all have heard the *Sweet Angels* song.
My old age is far too long, my youth was much too short.
For too long, this deathbed has been my fort,
I wish for my old bones to rest in the ground,
For my heart to not make a sound.
I pray for my soul to live in the sky
But the only way is for me to die.
On the other side, what's in store?
Will I find eternal peace, or endless war?
For me to know I must depart
And put an end to this old heart.
So, with my last heaving sigh
To those I love I say goodbye,
But let death not keep us apart.

37

Love?

Did something new happen to you?
I think it happened to me too.
I met you and you met me,
I guess it was just meant to be.

Time

Time is a stealthy creature
That makes a fool of all of us.
Like a bird, time flies and soars.
It can feel like your loyal dog,
But it's truly just a sly cat.

Time makes you think you have enough.
Sometimes it feels as slow as a turtle,
But truly it's like a cheetah,
Going by at blinding speed.

Time makes you think that it's your friend,
But as quiet as a fox, it leaves your side.
Unaware, you let the minutes pass.
Carelessly, you let the hours blow away
And now, your time is up.

I Know God Loves Me When...

I know God loves me when

His rain pours out from heaven to kiss my cheek.

I know God loves me when

His trees lift their long limbs to wave at me.

I know God loves me when

His sweet soft grass tickles my feet.

I know God loves me when

His sunshine stretches its arms out to hug me.

I know God loves me when

I say a small prayer and He answers me.

43

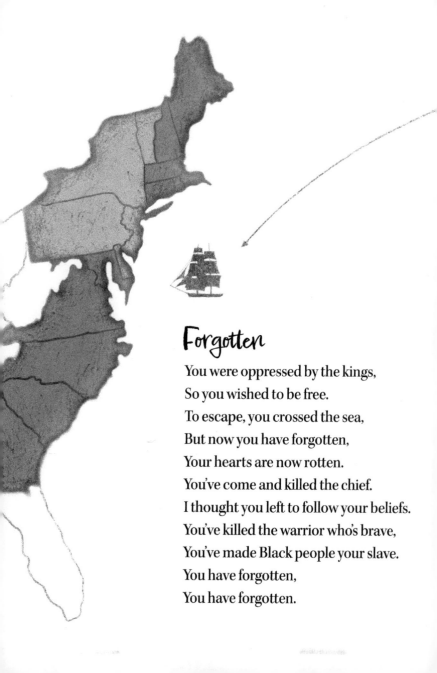

Forgotten

You were oppressed by the kings,
So you wished to be free.
To escape, you crossed the sea,
But now you have forgotten,
Your hearts are now rotten.
You've come and killed the chief.
I thought you left to follow your beliefs.
You've killed the warrior who's brave,
You've made Black people your slave.
You have forgotten,
You have forgotten.

45

Feeling Free

High up in the sky
There's no exact way to fly.
Picking a flower from a cloud tree
Or diving through cotton pillows with glee
Up here, l am free to be me.

At Peace

Like the last rumblings of a rusty engine,
A lonely wanderer draws his last breath from this world.
His small voice is drowned out for good,
Life is something of the past for him.
He is finally at peace.

49

A Child's Soul

A child's soul is as free as a bird.

Without a care in the world,

With no thought of sorrow.

Cages are nothing to them, because they can fly.

But every child grows and their soul grows with them.

They soon forget how to be free,
Cages now trap them in.
And they long for the time
When cages opened at their command.
Their wings have been clipped,
But not mine, I am free.

A Mother and Her Baby

The light of the moon shines upon your wispy hair,
Your soft giggles play with the silence of the night.
I do not need to look up at the sky to see the stars
For in your curious eyes I see all the twinkles
Of the universe and a thousand more.

The cold is biting me for it is a winter night,
To have you all to myself, I could stand here for hours.
I promise I will keep you warm my little one,
Though it is the coldest of nights.

53

NATURE

Unspoken Wisdom

You were there in the beginning,
You were forged by magma and stone.
You have been worn by the four winds
And all the sand of the desert.

You have seen love flourish and wilt,
You have seen birth and death,
You have known war and peace,
You have silently watched history
Unfold before your eyes.

Now look upon me
Oh rock of centuries past,
And tell me what you know.
Stay silent no longer, I beg,
Let your wisdom pour out like a flood.
Let the tapestry of years unravel for me to see.

As always, you are silent,
You turn a deaf ear,

I must learn on my own.
Like all the others before me,
You'll watch my life begin and see it end.
Peace, love, and death,
Time and time again, forever more.

The Wind

I love the wind,
On a sunny spring day,
It tickles you like something funny
And it tastes as sweet as honey.
Across the cities, across the plains,
It smells like a summer shower before it rains.
On a crisp fall day, it smells of pumpkin spice and apple pie,
And it whisks and swirls the dying leaves up high.
On a chilly winter day, it brings the taste of candy cane
And decorations to every window pane.
I love the wind, its everywhere,
It is in the trees and in my hair.

Papaya

This strange fruit of orange and black
It seems to have millions of beady little eyes.
Is it staring at me?
Because I am staring at it!

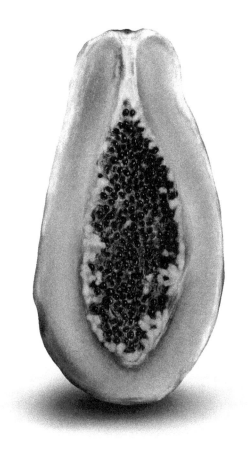

61

Ocean

Swish and sway your waters say.
When I get near, foam comes my way.
Under your waters, I see fish play.
I can smell your lovely ocean spray
In your glassy water seaweed sways.
I see whales swimming in your bay.
The seagulls at play say "Hey!"
So, you would understand why I want to stay
But now I must go, bye ocean, see you another day.

63

Luna

As I see the moon up in the sky
I really wish that I could fly,
So I could touch the moon's soft glow.
Why can't I go?
Tell me, tell me, I want to know.

Kissing Stars

Where the sky and the sea kiss
Two stars are born,
One in the sky
And one in the sea.

67

Kissed by Rain

The most delicate roses and the most stubborn weeds
Are kissed by rain.
The saddest willows and the happiest maple trees
Are kissed by rain.
The softest grass and the roughest hay
Are kissed by rain.
The tiniest puddles and the largest water ways
Have all been kissed by rain.

Hue to Hue

Every tone of red and yellow ranging from hue to hue.
This fish is something beautiful for me and you.

Forget Me Not

Forget me not, forget me not.

Like the most beautiful of flowers fading from blue to violet

Forget me not,

Like the smell that drifts from the most enchanting flower

Forget me not,

Like the pentagon of perfection that binds each petal of melting purple and blue

Forget me not,

Like the tangled net of vines that seems to knit its way upon the land,

Forget me not, forget me not.

73

A Fairy and an Orchid

I awaken in your slipper,
I unfurl your petals like a zipper,
I quietly dress in leaves so fine,
I go up your stem and at the top I dine.

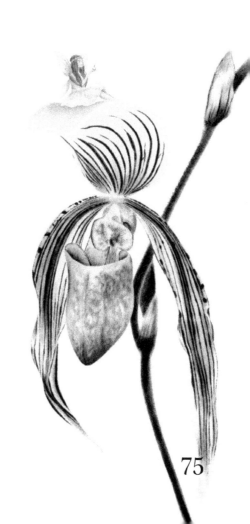

75

Crazy Fruit

I see a pear in underwear,
I see an apple praying in a chapel.
I spy a peach with a pie in reach,
I see a grape stealing tape,
I see a cherry that is hairy,
I see a banana with its nana,
I see an orange...
Well, there is no rhyme for him.

Blooming

Both sun and rain have helped you grow

In your egg of petals you are safe from wind and snow.

Now time has passed and you're the first to bloom.

Spread your purple petals, like a bird, fly away from winter's doom.

At Springs End

At springs end
The fierce tiger lily is sold.
At springs end
The peonies finally unfold.
At springs end
The zinnias are big and bold.
At springs end
The alyssum is in every valley fold.
At springs end
All children have a dahlia to hold.

A World of Difference

A world with no moon nor a sun,
Could it be fun?
I bet the water would float
So, you could fly a boat?
Then the sky would sink.
A cool place, don't you think?
A dark space with no pinks, greens or even blue
But what if everyone flew?
Then they would all squawk like birds
So no words, yet all are heard

83

Above

Stars above look like little twinkles of love
Like glimmers of hope in an endless sky.
Five spiked points in our imagination,
But in science they are big balls of fire, lit by an eternal fuel.

I imagine dark halls constructed by empty space
With stars dancing and twinkling in them.
I think they are embroidered into the sky
And are made with tears of joy
That happened to float up high.

A FEW HAIKUS

I

In a snow dipped land,
Quiet and still, with a cry
Proud bird shakes the earth.

II

Our water blessed land
Filled with majestic nature,
Here the salmon flow.

III

Our country's symbol
Looks down at all it protects,
Soaring among clouds.

IV

For these simple fish
Life's a fight for all its kind.
Home is their life's rest.

V

Predator and prey,
For one death, means life goes on.
Still, for one life's lost.

VI

Hi, hummingbird small,
Hummingbird swift and vibrant
On nectar you dine.

VII

River blue and cold,
Talons sharp, eagle soars proud
Run salmon, life's short.

A FEW MORE POEMS

Looks Like

Soap bubbles look like coffee foam
And tree bark looks like crocodiles.
I have a list of things that look like other things,
It could go on for miles.
South America and Africa look like two left feet,
Rubies look like mini beets,
Winter clouds look like blankets,
And snakes look like funny bracelets.

Pasta looks like hair
And big pillows look like bears.
Music notes look like bugs
And tongues look like wet rugs.
Curly hair looks like telephone cords
And paper looks like small floors.
Soap bubbles look like coffee foam
And tree bark looks like crocodiles.

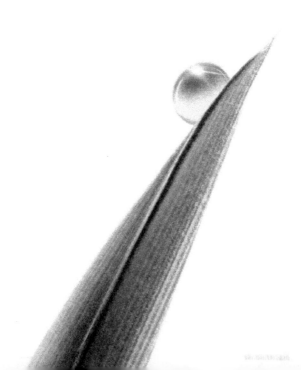

Jewels Everywhere

Dewy grass is not just water plopped on long strands of green,
It's small diamonds drizzled on fine lines of emerald glass.
Snow is not just frozen water from the cloudy sky,
It's powdered pearls lightly dusted onto earth.
At first glance you may not see all there is to see,
Truly look and you will find hidden jewels everywhere.

In Perfect Harmony

It's sometimes called a fiddle,
And is usually very little.
There's a frog on the bow
And four strings down the middle.
They know the same song
So, they both play along.

A Swan? A Rose?

A swan?
A rose?
Feathers as white as milk
Petals white as snow
Arching neck so delicate
Bending steam so frail
Sheading feather taken by the wind
Wilting petal blown away by the breeze
A swan?
A rose?

Execution

I fear so much my fait
Next is a cruelty so great
Worry has seized my hunger
They won't fail in deformity, in killing no blunder
Now I dread
Soon I shall fall dead
Now my heart cries
Fear to me ties
Heart beat quickens
Stomach sickens
Soon I shall be at the stake
But I won't tremble for honors sake
Almost time for the deed to be done
From death I cannot run
My life has brought me here
My final memory comes back a tear

Poverty

Poverty! Poverty!
You are what tears a family
You make the lowly tremble
You are the fear that makes great men disassemble
You are the whip that slashes the backs of the poor
You close all of opportunities doors
A rock in the shoe of all
You stir tensions and create brawls

Poverty I wish you would go away!
But like evil tar stuck you stay
Stuck, in a broken man's mind
You make the eyes of judgement blind
When you are around good is forgotten
Hopes become ash and go rotten
You send the thief out into the night
With you, children don't get a bite
The plague of humanity
The scourge of every country
Oh, Poverty! Poverty!

Life of the sun

The sun rises and to light it gives birth
Its young morning rays stroke the earth
Bright is the brand-new dawn
The birds serenade the sun with their song
Slowly the sun grows in the sky
To childish dreams it waves goodbye
Now it has much work to do
The sun's thinks only of keeping alive our dot of blue
So much time of hard work has made it weary
The ageing sun falls tiered and dreary
Its light weakens and darkness seeps
Dark death overtakes and the sun finally sleeps

Morning

Eyes flutter open
The sun still like a small crystal token
A breath breaks the silence so long unbroken
Dreams wished to be kept quickly chosen
Life grows in the morning air
Heavy limbs lift here now there
Quiet steps placed with care
Tiptoes dance swiftly down the stairs
Breakfast smells drift to the nose
Scents of waking coffee, orange, and summer rose
Morning breeze now more harshly blows
Hungry child downstairs goes

111

Printed in the USA
CPSIA information can be obtained
at www.ICGtesting.com
LVHW050023030224
770831LV00073B/1705